W9-CZW-035

Leadership Skills & Character Building
TOLERANCE & COOPERATION

TITLES IN THE SERIES

- **Communication Skills**
- **Initiative, Grit & Perseverance**
- **Integrity & Honesty**
- **Organization & Problem-Solving**
- **Self-Confidence**
- **Self-Discipline & Responsibility**
- **Tolerance & Cooperation**

Leadership Skills & Character Building

TOLERANCE & COOPERATION

Sarah Smith

MASON CREST

Mason Crest
450 Parkway Drive, Suite D
Broomall, Pennsylvania PA 19008
(866) MCP-BOOK (toll free)

First printing
9 8 7 6 5 4 3 2 1

ISBN: 978-1-4222-4001-4
Series ISBN: 978-1-4222-3994-0
ebook ISBN: 978-1-4222-7792-8

Cataloging-in-Publication Data on file with the Library of Congress.

Printed and bound in the United States of America.

QR CODES AND LINKS TO THIRD-PARTY CONTENT

Contents

KEY ICONS TO LOOK FOR:

Words to Understand: These words with their easy-to-understand definitions will increase the reader's understanding of the text while building vocabulary skills.

Sidebars: This boxed material within the main text allows readers to build knowledge, gain insights, explore possibilities, and broaden their perspectives by weaving together additional information to provide realistic and holistic perspectives.

Educational Videos: Readers can view videos by scanning our QR codes, providing them with additional content to supplement the text. Examples include news coverage, moments in history, speeches, iconic sports moments, and much more!

Text-Dependent Questions: These questions send the reader back to the text for more careful attention to the evidence presented there.

Research Projects: Readers are pointed toward areas of further inquiry connected to each chapter. Suggestions are provided for projects that encourage deeper research and analysis.

Series Glossary of Key Terms: This back-of-the-book glossary contains terminology used throughout the series. Words found here increase the reader's ability to read and comprehend higher-level books and articles in this field.

INTRODUCTION: INSPIRATION TO THE READER

The most effective leaders have a combination of intellectual intelligence (IQ), technical skills, and emotional intelligence (EI). Emotional intelligence is an essential ingredient. EI is the act of knowing, understanding, and responding to emotions, overcoming stress in the moment, and being aware of how your words and actions affect others. Emotional intelligence consists of five attributes: self-awareness, self-management, empathy, motivation, and effective communication.

The Unrelenting Athlete

> *"I've missed more than 9000 shots in my career. I've lost almost 300 games. Twenty-six times I've been trusted to take the game winning shot and missed. I've failed over and over and over again in my life. And that is why I succeed."*
> —Michael Jordan

The Bold Poets

> *"I've learned that people will forget what you said, people will forget what you did, but people will never forget how you made them feel."*
> —Maya Angelou

> *"What's money? A man is a success if he gets up in the morning and goes to bed at night and in between does what he wants to do."*
> —Bob Dylan

Becoming more confident as a leader in any capacity will help you inspire others and set a positive example. Gaining confidence in yourself, and finding more joy and peace of mind as you go about life, will help you handle all the successes, challenges, and setbacks along the way. Inside the pages of this book we will discuss all the components to improving your leadership skills, bringing you more confidence and building your character to become the leader you want to be some day.

The Inspiring Creators

> *"Whether you think you can or you think you can't, you're right."*
> —Henry Ford

> *"Strive not to be a success, but rather to be of value."*
> —Albert Einstein

The Captivating Writer

> *"Twenty years from now you will be more disappointed by the things that you didn't do than by the ones you did do, so throw off the bowlines, sail away from safe harbor, catch the trade winds in your sails. Explore. Dream. Discover."*
> —Mark Twain

Words to Understand

abstract: not concrete; theoretical

intelligence: the ability to learn and understand

intimidate: to frighten, especially by threats

Oprah Winfrey has overcome a challenging childhood to become an inspiration, not just to African Americans, but to everyone. Her courage, wisdom, and genuine nature is revered by all genders, races and ages alike. Her leadership skills have earned her the respect of millions worldwide.

Chapter One
HOW TOLERANCE & COOPERATION CAN BUILD CHARACTER & LEADERSHIP SKILLS

In schools across North America, a lot of time is spent helping children and teens develop intellectual **intelligence**, critical reasoning, **abstract** thinking, and other standard measures of academic success. Of course, there's good reason for this. Our ever-changing world needs future leaders who are educated, knowledgeable, and insightful.

But the world *also* needs leaders who are tolerant, compassionate, cooperative, and able to engage positively with others—even when their political, social, and religious beliefs differ. These are the leaders who can unite instead of divide, inspire instead of **intimidate**, and, ultimately, effect meaningful change rather than just push the status quo.

The main message of this book hinges on the belief that while a good leader must demonstrate a large number of traits, tolerance and cooperation are absolutely key.

Why Tolerance & Cooperation Are Important to the Effective Leader

Tolerance, or the willingness to accept something (especially if a person does not necessarily agree with it), is a sign of maturity and poise. Cooperation, or the ability to work well with others, is also a sign of maturity, and requires a great many interpersonal skills, such as communication and empathy. Both of these traits can help a leader be more successful in terms of making an impact, achieving a goal, completing a mission, and guiding others.

How Tolerance & Cooperation Can Build Character & Leadership Skills

Good leaders in the military have to show many qualities, including acceptance, cooperation, collaboration, responsibility, and honesty. Service personnel can at times find themselves in dangerous situations, where reliance on a good leader can be the difference between life or death.

Like intellectual intelligence, tolerance and cooperation can be developed over time. This is important, because it means that, while some people certainly have a natural penchant to lead, leaders are not just born. Anyone can develop the skills necessary to influence and manage other people successfully.

Specifically, leaders of a given unit, business, or organization who routinely exhibit tolerance and cooperation can establish an environment of open-mindedness and teamwork, which benefits the group as a whole. Tolerant and cooperative leaders also stand to gain greater insight and more information from their teammates, associates, business rivals, customers, and anyone else they interact with on a regular basis. This can help them accumulate knowledge, gain a competitive edge within their given field, and innovate creatively.

Lastly, tolerance and cooperation are essential traits of the good leader because they can help expand the leader's circle of influence. The more people that a leader can positively inspire, influence, and empower, the greater his or her impact on their local and global community will be.

What to Expect From This Book

This book is intended to help students understand and cultivate necessary social and leadership skills that aren't always explicitly discussed in the classroom. When combined with the more typical academic skills developed throughout a student's school career, these traits have the potential to create the type of world leaders that future generations can truly depend on.

Each chapter discusses critical topics and highlights real-world examples that can help teens and young adults understand how traits such as acceptance, cooperation, collaboration, responsibility, and honesty can be applied in a variety of ways to help them succeed. This success can be found not only in their future careers but also in other areas of life, including personal relationships and even mental well-being.

First, students will be introduced to the concepts of tolerance and cooperation through the lens of politics, human rights, and other important global topics. They'll learn about how the media has a heavy influence on these topics, and how they, as aspiring leaders, can appropriately make sense of all the information with fairness and understanding.

Students will also see how tolerance and cooperation can be applied to sensitive but important topics like race, religion, and culture. These big-picture concepts

Poverty to Wealth: Mahatma Gandhi

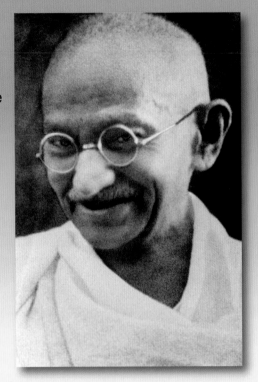

Few other people from history are as synonymous with peace and tolerance as Mahatma Gandhi (1869–1948). Born in India, Gandhi was a leader in the South Asian country's movement for independence from British rule. He showed the world that through nonviolence, peaceful protest, personal sacrifice, and a steadfast belief in one's rights, powerful change could occur on a large scale.

Among his many inspiring acts of tolerance and cooperation, Gandhi created an *ashram* (similar to a church) that was open to all the people of India, a country divided by an intricate caste system that many critics say promotes unjust treatment and discrimination. Gandhi was also well known for fasting and performing hunger strikes as a way to raise awareness about social issues of civil liberty and human rights within his country and the world at large. He inspired and unified millions of people through his belief that truth and discipline are at the heart of any healthy act of civil disobedience and fight for justice.

Sadly, Gandhi was assassinated in 1948. His legacy of simplicity, humility, tolerance, and compassion live on to this day. As the leader famously said, "Be the change you wish to see in the world."

must be dealt with tactfully by the effective leader in any field, especially in a world where tensions within these areas are higher than ever.

The book will then transition from a macro to a more micro scale. That is, tolerance and cooperation will be discussed as they apply to personal relationships, including with colleagues, teammates, friends, family members, and intimate partners. The student will see how their willingness to be more tolerant and cooperative will ultimately help them find success on both a professional and personal level.

At the end of this book, students should understand why character traits such as tolerance and cooperation are so critical for their success in the modern world. Hopefully, they'll also be empowered with the knowledge of *how* to develop these traits over the course of their academic career. This knowledge can help them as they prepare to enter the workplace and contribute (in ways both large and small) to their family, community, and society.

It's a big world we live in!

Text-Dependent Questions

1. Why should you be tolerant of other people's differences?

2. Why is cooperation critical to teamwork?

3. Where was Mahatma Gandhi born?

Research Project

Write a one-page essay on how tolerance and cooperation in the workplace can make a business successful.

Words to Understand

adversary: a person's opponent or rival in a contest, conflict, or dispute

diversity: the state of showing a great deal of variety and differences

human rights: rights that are believed to belong justifiably to every person and that are generally protected under local and international law

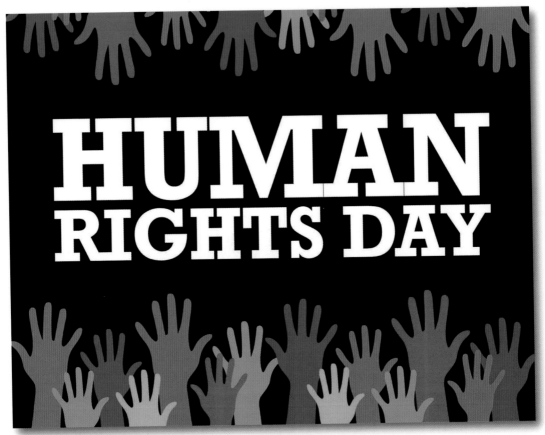

Human Rights Day is celebrated all over the world every year on December 10.

Chapter Two
POLITICS, HUMAN RIGHTS &
THE WORLD AROUND YOU

There may be no aspect of human experience that is more divisive and "hot button" as politics. Politicians and world leaders often disagree so strongly with each other that it becomes difficult to create, implement, or change policies affecting national and international law.

No matter what a person's political leanings are, however, it *is* possible to engage with an **adversary** in a collaborative way. Not only is this the best way to work together to create positive local and global change, but it also can help a person influence other people and garner more support for a movement or belief they care about.

Five Tips for Interacting With People Who Share Different Political Views

1. Be an Informed Citizen
A person who has clearly researched the candidates, topics, and policies that they care about will be able to formulate and develop their ideas more comprehensively, instead of just regurgitating something they heard on the news. This matters not just so that a person can "win an argument," but so he or she can properly advocate for their beliefs in a more respectful and effective way.

Make Your Voice Heard

The legal voting age in Canada and the United States is 18. By educating themselves about the candidates and topics up for vote, youths can make a big impact on their country and world. To register to vote in America, visit www.usa.gov/register-to-vote. To register to vote in Canada, visit https://ereg.elections.ca.

What Is Active Listening?

There are many resources available explaining what active listening is and how to practice it as a skill. Here are some of the key concepts, as outlined by the international organization Center for Creative Leadership: being quiet while the other person is talking, using positive body language, repeating and rephrasing what is being said, asking clarifying questions, and responding thoughtfully.

Nonviolent protests have been a part of political life for centuries. Protests can be used to inspire positive social change and advocate for the advancement of human rights.

2. Practice Active Listening

It's frustrating trying to communicate with someone who clearly isn't listening. A person who wants to effectively discuss opposing viewpoints should set the example of appropriate conduct by actively listening.

3. Avoid Personal Attacks

Disagreements over politics are normal, but people shouldn't let the conversation turn into attacks on the other person's character or worth. Set a firm boundary by not letting the discussion stray into volatile and intentionally hurtful territory. Instead, stick to discussing current events and debates.

4. Self-Regulate Emotions

It's normal to feel strong emotions about topics such as abortion, immigration, the military, the environment, tax reform, LGBT rights, and **human rights** violations. But if a person allows himself or herself to get carried away by their emotions, they may fail to communicate their beliefs effectively. Additionally, being able to monitor and manage emotions helps a person avoid the mistake of making personal attacks and saying things that are only intended to hurt other people.

What are universal human rights?

Keep an open mind by listening to a wide range of ideas and beliefs. Take time to evaluate what you have heard—you may surprise yourself at how your attitudes can change by listening to others.

5. Keep an Open Mind

People who are unable to see things from another perspective or are completely unwilling to change their mind about something rarely make good leaders. Plus, they may be missing out on new insights or a deeper understanding of complex issues. After all, not everyone fits neatly into one political party or belief system. A person can learn a lot by listening to someone else with genuine curiosity.

By keeping an open mind and trying to put themselves in the other person's shoes, a person can still stand up for his or her beliefs while at the same time treating other people with respect and dignity. An open-minded person can also tolerate the discomfort of having someone disagree with them—not everyone has to see things the same way! In fact, it's this kind of intellectual diversity that helps drive change in local, national, and international governments and communities.

Text-Dependent Questions

1. Name three cooperative ways you can interact with someone who shares a different political belief than you.

2. Why is it so important to regulate your emotions when having a discussion with someone you disagree with? Name one or two reasons.

3. Name two elements of active listening.

Research Project

Rewatch the video called "What Are the Universal Human Rights?" by Benedetta Berti of TED-Ed. The video is accessible at www.youtube.com/watch?v=nDgIVseTkuE. Then, do some research on the thirty articles listed in the Universal Declaration of Human Rights from the United Nations, available here: http://www.ohchr.org/EN/UDHR/Documents/UDHR_Translation s/eng.pdf. Write a one- to two-page essay on why you think universal human rights are important. Use specific rights as examples.

Words to Understand

bias: prejudice in favor of or against one thing, person, or group compared with another, usually in a way considered to be unfair

critical thinking: the ability to objectively analyze something in order to form a judgment or opinion

skepticism: a philosophical stance and an attitude of doubting (not necessarily denying) the truth of commonly held beliefs or knowledge

Nowadays, more of us are accessing our daily news online via our laptops, tablets, and smartphones. Despite this, a good number of us still like to read a traditional newspaper to get our news.

Chapter Three
USING NEWSPAPERS & OTHER MEDIA TO UNDERSTAND THE WORLD AROUND YOU

As mentioned in the previous chapter, being an informed and educated citizen is one of the best ways that a person can cooperate and interact positively with other people, especially people who do not share the same political beliefs. After all, it can be difficult for two groups of people (or countries or organizations, etc.) to come together in unity if they are basing their beliefs and perspectives of each other off of misinformation or distorted facts.

But finding the right resources to help form a person's knowledge and belief system can be challenging. Many of the mainstream media sources (including social media) show political and ideological **bias**. Coverage of a single current event on one website can have an entirely different headline, slant, and tone compared to another website. It's especially true when comparing news sources from one country to another.

The problem is that this can cause a well-meaning person to form an opinion based on something that is inaccurate, exaggerated, or even untrue. For this reason, it's important to use many different sites and sources when trying to develop an understanding about something. Using a quality fact-checking resource can be instrumental in becoming an informed citizen and voter.

The Best Unbiased Fact-Checking Websites

Students, business owners, and other leaders need accurate and valid sources to help them make informed

Using Newspapers & Other Media to Understand the World Around You

decisions. The following websites are renowned for being independent, non-partisan, responsible, and reliable:

- **AllSides:** www.allsides.com
- **FactCheck:** www.factcheck.org
- **Open Secrets:** www.opensecrets.org
- **PolitiFact:** www.politifact.com
- **ProPublica:** www.propublica.org
- **Snopes:** www.snopes.com
- **The Sunlight Foundation:** www.sunlightfoundation.com

Most news organizations are biased toward one political leaning. For this reason, make time to read a selection of news sources. This will help you form your opinions and broaden your horizons.

Fact or Fiction?

According to psychological research, some of the benefits of healthy skepticism include:

- protection against misleading information,
- promotion of increased political awareness and involvement, and
- an increased ability to form unique opinions and insights.

Be a Healthy Skeptic

In addition to making sure their sources are accurate and fair, a good leader will make sure that they approach every new idea or situation with a healthy amount of **skepticism**. This helps prevent a person from simply falling for biased coverage in the media as well as from accepting any blanket statement as fact without actually determining if it's true (this is especially important if the so-called "fact" is really just someone's strong opinion instead).

Here area few helpful questions from the American Press Institute that a person can ask to help them know if a particular news or media source is trustworthy:

What Kind of Content Is This? For instance, is this an opinion piece? An editorial? A journalistic news piece? The

Sometimes, it is possible that you will inadvertently read what is known as "fake news." This is inaccurate, sometimes sensationalistic reporting designed to mislead, deceive, or damage a persons reputation—so be wary.

For some people, it is a sad situation that the shift to digital news, a decline in newspaper advertising, and changes in reading habits have led to the decline in the circulation of traditionally printed newspapers.

Social Media Is the New News

Decades ago, there were only a few news stations, newspapers, and radio programs for people to get their news from. These days, news can be found all over the Internet and social media—and lots of it, too. According to research carried out in 2016, 57 percent of Americans got their news from TV, 38 percent from social media and other websites, 25 percent from radio, and 20 percent from printed newspapers.

Coming to an incorrect conclusion. By Carl Sagan

first two types of content tend to put forward an argument about something, although a news article in a partisan publication can be quite biased, too.

Who and What Are the Sources Cited and Why Should I Trust Them? Does the piece reference a subject expert, an eyewitness, a politician, or a research organization? Is this person or organization being funded by anyone? Is this source biased? Are they reliable? For example, an eyewitness reporting on an event that happened a long time ago may have faulty memory.

What's the Evidence? Evidence is the proof that sources present to support their argument and it shows whether or not their argument is valid or true. The more specific and transparent a news piece is about the evidence and sources it uses, the more likely it is you can trust it. Circling or highlighting evidence and other key points as you read an article can be a helpful exercise.

Are the Conclusions of the Piece Supported by the Evidence? Is the main takeaway being logically drawn from the evidence? Or are assumptions and speculations being made?

What's Missing? Are there any holes in the story that are unexplained or confusing?

Am I Learning What I Need? An informed citizen should be able to explain a subject they're interested in to someone else. This helps a person make sure that the media they consume is worthwhile and beneficial to them.

Today, with instant global media coverage, news can arrive on our smartphone or TV before the true facts have been established. In some cases, once the true facts emerge, the original reporting is shown to be inaccurate.

Ultimately, a person's own thoughts and behaviors are their own responsibility. People should do their best to ensure that they use their **critical thinking** skills and are basing their beliefs off of valid facts, logic, and reason. They should also be willing to change their minds if new valid information becomes available.

Good leaders and good citizens must be able to think critically about complex current events in order to avoid becoming swept up by the fearmongering that is so prevalent in today's modern media. This is the key for practicing and maintaining a healthy level of tolerance and acceptance day to day.

Text-Dependent Questions

1. What does "bias" mean?

2. Why is it helpful to use fact-checking resources when learning about a current event?

3. Name two questions you can ask yourself when reading an article or listening to a news story in order to help you figure out if it's trustworthy.

Research Project

Do some research on how to improve your critical thinking skills. A video called "5 Tips to Improve Your Critical Thinking" by Samantha Agoos of TED-Ed is a great start. The video is available here:
www.youtube.com/watch?v=dItUGF8GdTw
Next, head to one of the top fact-checking websites named in this chapter and choose an article about a topic that interests you. Then, write a one-page report summarizing the piece. Be sure to talk about the sources used, evidence cited, and conclusions drawn.

Words to Understand

marginalized: a person, group, or concept treated as insignificant or peripheral

prejudiced: having a preconceived opinion that is not based on reason or actual experience; dislike, hostility, or unjust behavior that comes from unfounded opinions

stereotypes: widely held but fixed and oversimplified images or ideas of a particular type of person or thing

A well-integrated community values the differences in people and embraces those from different backgrounds. The benefit is that people can come together from different races, nationalities, religions, and sexes to coexist in harmony.

Chapter Four
THE IMPORTANCE OF RACIAL & RELIGIOUS TOLERANCE

Look around: different cultures, races, ethnicities, and religions can be found all over the globe—and even within a single town, apartment building, or classroom! This diversity of human appearance, language, culture, and creativity has contributed to much of the world's best art, technological advances, and social movements (and, unfortunately, much of the war and turmoil as well). Tolerance is key to engaging in all of these different and sometimes unfamiliar cultures in a dignified and collaborative way.

Recall that to be tolerant, a person does not necessarily have to adopt the beliefs and values of another person. Instead, the tolerant person can respect and live peacefully among people who live or think differently than they do (that is, as long as their beliefs do not infringe upon anyone else's basic rights, property, or safety).

The Importance of Racial & Religious Tolerance

    Effective leaders (of nations, organizations, businesses, and even families) should strive toward a standard of tolerance for people not only with different political beliefs but with different religious beliefs and lifestyles as well. This can foster a sense of unity and connection, which may very well be needed on a global scale in order to manage many of the problems affecting our planet.

Top Dos & Don'ts When It Comes to Race, Religion, Sexual Orientation & Other Personal Characteristics

DON'T Speak or Behave With Prejudice

Using hateful words, making rude gestures, telling or retelling racial or offensive jokes—let alone inflicting violence—are simply all unacceptable behaviors from

We should all learn to respect and celebrate the differences in all people and, despite how we look, dress, eat, or celebrate, we are all human beings and therefore should be proud of our diversity.

Can You Have Prejudice and Not Know It?

Psychologists from several American universities have created a series of implicit association tests that can help a person recognize any hidden biases they may have (these are often copied from our parents and other authority figures). To take your own test, go to this website: https://implicit.harvard.edu/implicit/.

anyone who wishes to make a positive and inspiring impact on the world and the people around them.

DON'T Turn a Blind Eye to Bullies

It takes a courageous person to stand up to a bully, especially if the bully is teasing, making fun of, or threatening someone else they consider to be "different." In fact, bullies are the perfect example of what it means *not* to be courageous and cooperative leaders.

Nobody should tolerate words, behavior, or policies that harm other people or take away someone's rights. If someone is being bullied, speak up.

DO Practice Cultural Sensitivity

Cultural sensitivity is not only the belief that "I can accept people who are different than me," but also that "people who are different than me are okay." In other words, it's perfectly okay for someone to believe, act, dress, and speak in a different way provided that their beliefs and actions don't harm them or anyone else, or infringe upon a person's basic human rights.

Practicing cultural sensitivity, then, means not making fun of someone for the way they look or for what they believe. A culturally sensitive person also treats others the way they would want to be treated, regardless of their race, gender, age, sexual orientation, and so on.

A culturally sensitive person does not just assume that all the **stereotypes** about different types of people are true. This person also understands that everyone they interact with has a completely different life experience and perspective that is as valid as his or her own.

The Importance of Racial & Religious Tolerance

What does every human really want?

It can be very interesting to research your family ancestry. By looking back through old records, you may be surprised by how much information you can find and how fascinating it is.

DO Ask Questions

Young students must be curious about their world. After all, someday they will be contributing to their larger society through work, travel, volunteerism, and maybe even parenting. So learning how to ask good questions is critical to understanding more of the world and the many different types of people in it.

If a person wants to learn more about a different culture, race, or religion, they should try to find opportunities to meet and interact with people from that particular group. This is especially true in the modern world, where information shared in the media and on the Internet (as discussed earlier) may not always be as reliable or factual as it seems.

Being curious, open-minded, and accepting is much more beneficial to society than remaining biased, **prejudiced**, and discriminatory. After all, humans are much more alike than it may seem, and practicing compassion and respect for one's neighbors can help make communities feel safer as a whole.

DO Show Pride in Your Own Culture and Family History

As well as learning more about other cultures, try to learn about your own. This can create a feeling of belonging, which is an important part of human nature. But it can also serve as a valuable point of discussion about how harmful discrimination (of ethnic minorities, women, immigrants, and so on) was in the past. And by examining the past we get a better sense of how discrimination still operates today.

DO Focus on Personal Responsibility

As Gandhi said, "Be the change you wish to see in the world." If a person wants to live in a more peaceful, understanding, and accepting place, then they should make it a priority to become more peaceful, understanding, and accepting in their own actions first, instead of just blaming other people, the government, or

Bullying: Ethnicity, Race, and National Origin

Kids can get bullied because of their race, ethnicity, or national origin and there is an increasing awareness of this problem. Research shows that black and Hispanic teens who are bullied are more likely to suffer academically than their white peers.

The Importance of Racial & Religious Tolerance

society. This can set a worthy example to coworkers, friends, family members, and anyone else they may come in contact with, which can help spread the light of compassion, personal responsibility, and basic human decency.

Overall, the world as a whole, particularly in Western society, has made a lot of progress over the past few centuries as far establishing racial tolerance, cultural sensitivity, equality, and civil justice. Different groups of people who were once heavily **marginalized** by society (including women, people of color, and people who are gay or lesbian) have more and more equal standing in the eyes of the

Attitudes towards homosexuality vary greatly between different countries, cultures, and religions. However, in the West, same-sex relationships are now considered to be as conventional as heterosexual relationships. Despite these changing attitudes, prejudices still exist.

law. However, there are still many more strides to be taken and improvements to be made.

Now is a good time in history for younger generations to set the precedent of acceptance and tolerance for different beliefs, opinions, and cultures. This sense of unity could be the very thing needed for people to cooperate and work together "across party lines" in order to effect laws and policies that will promote fairness and justice for all.

Text-Dependent Questions

1. What is a stereotype?

2. Name one or two traits of a culturally sensitive person.

3. What does marginalization mean? Can you name a group of people who have been historically marginalized by their society?

Research Project

Write a reflective essay about common stereotypes that you think people may have about your own race, ethnicity, culture, gender, age, sexual orientation, political beliefs, or any other particular trait of yours. You could also write about common stereotypes about a person you know. Feel free to ask your teachers or parents for some guidance and help with developing your ideas. If you could tell people anything to help them understand you better, what you would you say? What would you want them to know? How are these stereotypes false? Is there any truth to them? Spend at least 20 to 30 minutes reflecting on these questions and writing down your thoughts.

Words to Understand

Communication: the imparting or exchanging of information or news; means of connection between people or places

emotional intelligence: the ability to be aware of, control, and express one's emotions, and to handle interpersonal relationships judiciously and empathetically

Empathy: the ability to understand and share the feelings of another

Having empathy is having the ability to understand other people's emotions. When you have a friend who is upset, show empathy by listening to their concerns without being judgmental. Offer your assistance if required and try to imagine how you would feel if you were in their shoes.

Chapter Five
UNDERSTANDING OTHER PEOPLE'S NEEDS

So far, a lot has been learned about how tolerance and cooperation are key to being an effective leader on a local, national, and international scale. Now it's time to narrow down the focus and understand how being more tolerant and cooperative can help a person lead and thrive within their more direct and personal relationships.

A Quotation to Ponder
"Do not judge another until you have walked a mile in their shoes."
—Native American Proverb

The Role of Empathy in Collaborative & Understanding Leadership

When it comes to understanding the needs of employees, colleagues, customers, friends, and family members, the personality trait of empathy plays a major role. Empathy, or the ability to understand and share the feelings of others, is essential for tolerance and cooperation. A leader of a business or family should be willing to try to see where a person is coming from (in other words, "put themselves in that person's shoes") in order to better understand what drives that person's behaviors, feelings, and thoughts. Empathy also helps a person understand what someone else needs. Why? Because people who demonstrate empathy tend to be better listeners and more effective communicators: not only can

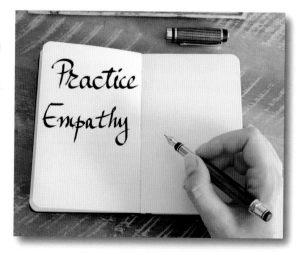

Understanding Other People's Needs

A good leader will show empathy by understanding the needs of his or her coworkers. If true empathy is shown, it will go a long way toward encouraging them to perform at their best.

they communicate their own needs better but they also tend to be more open and attentive to other people who are communicating with them.

Here are few other specific reasons (according to research) why being an empathetic leader is so crucial:

- An empathetic leader is easier to like and trust.
- Empathy helps a leader figure out the underlying reasons behind setbacks and challenges, which can help everyone learn from mistakes better.
- Being empathetic can help a leader resolve conflict by seeing both sides of an issue.
- Having empathy helps a person develop closer relationships (both professional and personal).

Tips for Improving Empathy

- Ask yourself why someone feels a certain way about something.
- Spend time with someone, or do something they usually do, to understand their experiences and point of view.
- Think about how you can change the way you interact with someone for the better.

So, how does one become more empathetic? It involves listening, being open-minded, and practicing the development of four key areas:

- The ability to adopt the perspective of another person
- Withholding judgment (for instance, not labeling someone)
- Recognizing the emotions of other people
- **Communication**

Of course, empathy is just one element of a tolerant and cooperative individual. A broader concept that can help explain why the best leaders inspire others is the theory of emotional intelligence. Unlike intellectual intelligence (IQ), which assesses how smart a person is, **emotional intelligence** (EQ or EI) refers to how well a person can recognize, manage, and influence their own emotions as well as the emotions of other people.

Five Self-Reflection Questions That Can Help Improve Emotional Intelligence

Emotional intelligence is made up of several components, including empathy. Here are five questions a person can ask themselves that will help them get a feel for their own level of emotional intelligence and assess how it changes and develops over time:

1. What Am I Feeling Right Now?
A person must be self-aware enough to understand and recognize what their own emotions are, especially if they want to be better at controlling them.

Understanding Other People's Needs

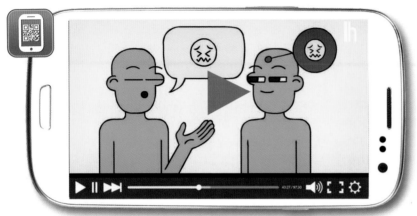

The importance of empathy

People with emotional intelligence know how to lead their coworkers in a productive manner. They can make informed decisions about things that matter the most while still nurturing their team.

Throughout our lives, almost all of us will experience times of stress. Consequently, it is wise to look at what we can do to control it. Sometimes, stress can be relieved simply by breathing deeply or taking a walk. However, if you feel that your stress levels are becoming out of control, it is important to seek help from a therapist or counsellor.

2. Why Do I Feel This Way?

In a moment of high emotions and stress, taking a time-out or a few deep breaths gives a person time to identify what factors are contributing to his or her strong feelings.

3. How Am I Coming Off to Other People?

Loved ones can shed an honest light on a person's behavior during times of high stress, which can help a person learn how to manage their emotions better. Helpful questions include, "Was I acting differently to you just now?" and "How did you feel about my actions?"

4. What Don't I Know About This Situation or Person?

Emotions are feedback tools that hint at underlying thoughts. If a person is exhibiting a strong emotion, it's probable that there are many factors contributing to his or her behavior, not all of which may be obvious. Is there anything from a person's life experience or current situation that could help explain why they are responding with such strong emotions?

Are You (Emotionally) Smart?

According to various research studies, the five key components or skills of emotional intelligence are self-awareness, managing emotions, self-motivation, empathy, and managing relationships. Like intellectual intelligence, these skills can be developed over time.

Good social skills enable us to form successful relationships, which not only give us pleasure but also influence our long-term health mental and physical health.

5. What Can I Learn From This?

Criticism and conflict are hard, but if a person learns from them they are not wasted. The leader who cares about cooperation and compassion will not get overly defensive in the face of critical feedback or disagreement. Instead, he or she will ask: "Leaving my personal feelings out of this, what can I learn from this experience? How can I use this information to help me and my team/loved ones improve next time?" Understand that being emotionally intelligent, empathetic, and communicative are key ingredients in developing better leadership skills at school, in the workplace, and even in personal relationships.

Text-Dependent Questions

1. What does empathy mean?

2. What are the five basic areas of emotional intelligence that a person can develop?

3. Why do people with emotional intelligence make good leaders?

Research Project

Communication is essential to being able to understand what a person's needs are. Read this article from Psych Central: https://psychcentral.com/lib/become-a-better-listener-active-listening/. You can also refer to the side bar shared earlier in Chapter Two. Be sure to jot down some notes. Then, have a conversation with a friend, family member, or other loved one. Focus on using a few active listening skills that you've learned about. After the conversation, write a one- to two-page essay about your experience. How did your active listening change the conversation? Was it difficult to do? How do you think your active listening affected the other person?

Words to Understand

cooperation: the process of working together to the same end

delegate: to entrust a task or responsibility to another person

diplomatic: having or showing an ability to deal with people in a sensitive and effective way

At school or college it is usual that you will have to work on a group project with other students. This group of young architecture students are working together on some drawings.

Chapter Six
LEARNING TO WORK WITH OTHERS

Building empathy, communication skills, listening skills, and emotional intelligence will help a leader learn how to be more sensitive to the needs of others, even people who are very different from them. To take it one step further, however, a good leader must also be able to recognize and respond to a person's needs in order to promote effective interaction and help people work together.

In other words, awareness and understanding are important bits of knowledge to have, but *acting* on this knowledge through teamwork and collaboration is essential.

Learning Together Through Cooperation

Very often in school, students are asked to complete group assignments and projects. Many students also work together on athletic teams or in clubs. In all these situations, it's helpful to have some tools that will allow students from all walks of life to come together in **cooperation** for a common goal.

Many teachers and researchers have found that cooperative learning is an effective way to improve understanding and maximize personal and group achievement. Here are five key ways to improve a group's cooperation:

1. Understand the unique contribution that each group member can make.
2. Make sure each person is assigned (and completes) their fair share of work; **delegate** tasks appropriately, according to the relative strengths and abilities of each group member.

Half a Dozen is the Sweet Spot

Research tends to show that a team of four to six people is optimal for any sort of group project or mission. Four- to six-person teams tend to be more cooperative, productive, and united toward the common goal of the group.

Have you ever felt that it is easier to do the work yourself than give it to someone else to do? In the world of work, a leader will be required to delegate to other employees. This is something that all leaders will have to learn to do.

When working as a team, it is important that all members are able to express their opinions and views.

3. Practice how to share and communicate ideas in an effective way among the group
4. Reflect on both the group and individual performance; for instance, asking questions like "Was the objective achieved effectively?"
5. Build on group and individual reflection, this step asks team members to practice emotional intelligence and resolve any lingering conflicts or challenges

Teachers and leaders can help facilitate cooperative learning among students, colleagues, and other peers. However, it should also be the individual student's responsibility to practice cooperation and communication skills in order to improve their experience, as well as the group dynamic as a whole.

Learning to Work With Others

In a work environment it is not uncommon to have disagreements, particularly if the other coworkers are passionate about the work in hand. If a conflict arises, take the initiative to try to calm the situation. Listen to the other person's views and, if applicable, try to compromise.

How to deal with conflict

Learning & Working Together

Research has shown that cooperative learning offers a variety of benefits to students, including: increased confidence, improved critical thinking skills, and an improved sense of respect and appreciation for fellow students and the learning process itself.

Helpful Tips for Dealing With Conflict

Conflict and disagreement aren't necessarily a bad thing when working with others. In fact, if handled with tact and understanding, conflict can actually help a team achieve more.

Additionally, conflict is normal and likely to occur when working together on a team or in a group. Here are a few helpful tips to make sure that any team, group, or family deals with inevitable conflict in a more productive and cooperative way:

Practice Empathy

As mentioned in the last chapter, empathy not only makes a person a more effective leader who can understand and recognize a person's needs but it can also help a person resolve conflict faster. A person in conflict should stop and try to see things from the other person's perspective before digging in their heels and rigidly sticking to their own feelings and points of view. This will automatically improve listening skills and facilitate cooperation.

As author Stephen Covey wrote in his bestselling book, *The 7 Habits of Highly Effective People*, "seek first to understand, then to be understood."

Be Diplomatic

Use words, body language, and a tone of voice that conveys understanding and sensitivity toward another person. This can be hard to do if the other person is being emotionally reactive or overly critical. But self-control

By being cooperative and understanding at work, the relationships between coworkers will be more effective and harmonious.

over one's own emotions and behaviors is a great thing to practice, and an important skill to have that can be useful in school, at work, and at home.

Take a Time-Out
Sometimes, temporarily removing oneself from a conflict situation is the best strategy. It gives people time to calm down and gain some perspective on the situation. Then, the team members can come back later in a more balanced and cooperative state of mind.

Take Personal Responsibility
Don't make excuses for poor behavior. If a mistake has been made, own it. If necessary, apologize (and forgive). Being willing to take responsibility for one's own actions is a strong sign of leadership and may help inspire others on the team to do the same (which can end the useless "blame-and-shame game").

Whether a team's goal is to complete an assignment, sell a product, pass a law, or even simply run a household, the team leaders must be able to inspire people to work together. In this sense, *everyone* on the team can be considered a leader!

Of course, it's not reasonable to assume that a person will always get along with, or even like, someone that they are tasked to cooperate with. But by focusing on cooperation skills and learning how to be more **diplomatic** in interpersonal interactions, a person will be able to help create and maintain positive group dynamics and maximize the quality and efficiency of outcomes overall.

Text-Dependent Questions

1. What does it mean to be diplomatic?

2. Name three components of cooperative learning. Why is cooperative learning beneficial?

3. What are two ways that a person can handle conflict effectively?

Research Project

Think back to a time when you were working with someone on a project or activity that didn't go so well. Why did it not go well? Was there conflict? Miscommunication? Were the goals of the project not clear, or was the work not fairly shared? Identify in a few paragraphs what you felt were the factors contributing to those challenges and how they made you feel. Next, think back to a time when you were working on a group project that *did* go well. Why? Again, identify and write down your reflections in a few paragraphs.

bonds: ties that unite people; a common emotion or interest

compassion: concern for the sufferings or misfortunes of others

intimate: closely acquainted; familiar, close

Of course you love your parents—that's a given. Sometimes, our busy lives prevent us from spending as much time with them as we would like. However, as we get older the time we spend with our folks becomes more fulfilling. It is a opportunity to share memories and common interests.

Chapter Seven
FRIENDS & RELATIONSHIPS

Tolerance, cooperation, and empathy are essential to anyone who wants to lead a business, an organization, a government, a movement, or even a collaboration of world leaders.

But as important as it is to communicate and work together with people on a professional level, it's just as important to be communicative and cooperative with one's closest friends, family members, and loved ones. After all, these are the people with whom a person tends to share the closest emotional **bonds**. Great personal growth and development can come about thanks to **intimate** relationships, and research shows that having healthy and close friendships can improve mental health and even help people live longer.

Plus, it feels *good* to be kind to the ones we love.

Ten Ways to Be a Better Friend

Nobody should take for granted what it means to be a good friend. Here are a few helpful tips to keep in mind:

- Listen with empathy, patience, and compassion. Be there for one another.
- Be respectful and kind, even during disagreements. Be honest but not hurtful.
- Use physical affection to show caring and **compassion**.
- Give gifts that are meaningful and thoughtful (they can be large or small).
- Spend quality time with friends (put the cell phone away!). Show an interest in the things they like.
- Do kind things and be helpful.

Want to Live Longer? Make a Buddy

A study done by researchers at the University of Utah found that having strong social relationships can increase a person's odds of survival by as much as 50 percent. This is comparable to quitting smoking! It's been hypothesized that having good friends helps a person cope with stress better, find more meaning out of life, and encourage them to make healthier life choices.

Tolerant and cooperative people treat others how they would like to be treated themselves. As a consequence, they find it easier to form long-lasting relationships.

- Give compliments, and really mean them. Don't demand compliments in return.
- Do not try to change someone. Remember that everyone has "good" and "bad" traits.
- Be honest. Do not say or do cruel things toward a friend behind their back. Respect their privacy.
- Laugh and find humor in daily life.

These points all may seem like common sense but, oddly enough, sometimes people seem to be more patient and kind to complete strangers than they are to their own family members and friends. People who know each other well frequently know how to push each other's buttons. This is often because people are less tolerant of the so-called negative qualities of the people they spend the most time with. The "negative" qualities and traits that they see in their loved ones may remind them of the same qualities that they have in themselves but don't fully own or accept yet. To this extent, everyone around us is like a mirror, reflecting back parts of ourselves.

The simplest way to improve a relationship with someone is to remember the Golden Rule: *Treat others the way you yourself want to be treated.*

In Summary

This short book has been a guide that can help teens and young adults learn about what it means to be cooperative, tolerant, and understanding as they interact with

Know the difference between a good and bad friend

Cooperation: Good for Friends, Families & Partners

In a study published by the *Journal of Family Psychology*, researchers found that couples who end up getting divorced are more likely to use blame, negative criticism, and poor cooperation skills. The researchers also noted, however, that couples who had learned how to cooperate better with coaching and practice could improve their chances of maintaining a healthy relationship over time.

Friendship and true leadership are similar because both involve selflessness and concern for the well-being of others.

the people around them. In a world where conflict is as prevalent as ever, being able to see things from other people's perspectives, show empathy, listen effectively, and communicate clearly are critical skills that the future leaders of our planet need.

Maybe the hardest part about becoming more understanding and cooperative with others is committing to daily practice. It's not easy to change behaviors and thoughts. But with consistent practice and small daily steps, anyone can develop the emotional intelligence and tools necessary to be an inspiring, effective, and respected leader.

Text-Dependent Questions

1. Does having friends improve your chances of living longer? Why or why not?

2. Name three ways to be a good friend.

3. Rewatch the video in this chapter. What are three qualities of a "bad" friend? How do these contrast with the qualities of a "good" friend?

Research Project

Watch a favorite movie or television show. Knowing what you now know about being a good friend and about showing empathy, practicing tolerance, and being cooperative, identify a few relationships within the movie or TV show that demonstrate either good or bad qualities. Write about what you see and about how the relationships between these characters affects what happens in the story. Remember that a person can be a good friend sometimes and a bad friend at other times, too. Does this ever happen in the story? If so, how?

Series Glossary of Key Terms

ability	Power to do something.
addiction	A strong and harmful need to regularly have something (such as a drug).
anxiety	Fear or nervousness about what might happen.
argument	An angry disagreement.
assumption	Something accepted as true.
body language	Movements or positions of the body that express a person's thoughts or feelings.
challenge	A stimulating task or problem.
citizen	A person who lives in a particular place.
clarify	To make or become more easily understood.
collaborate	To work with others.
conclusion	Final decision reached by reasoning.
conflict	A clashing disagreement (as between ideas or interests).
confusion	Difficulty in understanding or in being able to tell one thing from a similar thing.
cooperation	The act or process of working together to get something done.
counsellor	A person who gives advice.
criticism	The act of finding fault.
culture	The habits, beliefs, and traditions of a particular people, place, or time.
discipline	Strict training that corrects or strengthens.
discriminate	To unfairly treat a person or group differently from other people or groups.
efficiency	The ability to do something or produce something without waste.
effort	Hard physical or mental work.
evidence	A sign which shows that something exists or is true.
experience	Skill or knowledge that you get by doing something.
feedback	Helpful criticism given to someone to indicate what can be done to improve something.
frustration	A feeling of anger or annoyance caused by being unable to do something.
goal	Something that you are trying to do or achieve.
grammar	The rules of how words are used in a language.
guarantee	A promise that something will be or will happen as stated.
guilt	A feeling of shame or regret as a result of bad conduct.
habit	A settled tendency or usual manner of behavior.
human right	A basic right that many societies believe every person should have.
humble	Not thinking of yourself as better than other people.
innovation	A new idea, method, or device.
inspiration	Something that moves someone to act, create, or feel an emotion.

interact	To talk or do things with other people.
intimidate	To make timid or fearful.
judgment	An opinion or decision that is based on careful thought.
manage	To take care of and make decisions about (someone's time, money, etc.).
maturity	The quality or state of being mature; especially full development.
media	The system and organizations of communication through which information is spread to a large number of people.
memory	The power or process of reproducing or recalling what has been learned and retained.
mindfulness	The practice of maintaining a nonjudgmental state of heightened or complete awareness of one's thoughts, emotions, or experiences.
mind-numbing	Very dull or boring.
motivation	The condition of being eager to act or work.
nutrition	The act or process of nourishing or being nourished.
opinion	Belief stronger than impression and less strong than positive knowledge.
opportunity	A favorable combination of circumstances, time, and place.
paper trail	Documents (such as financial records) from which a person's actions may be traced or opinions learned.
perspective	The ability to understand what is important and what isn't.
politics	The art or science of government.
ponder	To think about.
punctuation	The act or practice of inserting standardized marks or signs in written matter to clarify the meaning.
realistic	Ready to see things as they really are and to deal with them sensibly.
relationship	The state of interaction between two or more people, groups, or countries.
resolution	The final solving of a problem.
respect	To consider worthy of high regard.
retirement	Withdrawal of one's position or occupation or from active working life.
schedule	A written or printed list of things and the times when they will be done.
setback	A slowing of progress.
stress	A state of mental tension and worry caused by problems in your life, work, etc.
therapist	A person specializing in treating disorders or injuries of the body or mind, especially in ways that do not involve drugs and surgery.
trait	A quality that makes one person or thing different from another.
trust	To place confidence in someone or something.
valid	Based on truth or fact.

Further Reading & Internet Resources

Further Reading

Abrams, Irwin. *The Words of Peace: Selections From the Speeches of the Winners of the Nobel Peace Prize.* 4th edition. New York: Newmarket Press, 2008.

Brown, Brené. *Daring Greatly: How the Courage to Be Vulnerable Transforms the Way We Live, Love, Parent, and Lead.* New York: Penguin Random House, 2012.

Rau, Dana M. *Who Was Gandhi?* London: Penguin Workshop, 2014.

Sineck, Simon. *Start With Why: How Great Leaders Inspire Everyone to Take Action.* New York: Penguin Group, 2009.

Internet Resources

http://factcheck.org A website that strives to serve as a "nonpartisan, nonprofit 'consumer advocate' for voters that aims to reduce the level of deception and confusion" in politics. By confirming and reporting on the factual accuracy of things said and shared in the media, the website aims to promote better public understanding and awareness of policies, people, and events that affect our world.

https://canadafactcheck.ca Promising to give you "the real story behind Canada's news headlines," this Canadian version of PolitiFact is dedicated to "transparency, democratic reform, government accountability, and corporate responsibility."

https://www.bestbuddies.org This is the website of the nonprofit organization that aims to connect volunteers with people living with intellectual and developmental disabilities. Help special-needs kids, teens, and adults in your community find opportunities for one-on-one friendships, employment, and leadership development.

Organizations to Contact

United Nations
405 East 42nd Street
New York, NY 10017
Phone: 212-963-1234
Fax: 212-963-3133
Website: http://www.un.org

American Civil Liberties Union (ACLU)
125 Broad Street, 18th Floor
New York, NY 10004
Phone: 212-549-2500
Website: https://www.aclu.org

Canadian Civil Liberties Association (CCLA)
90 Eglinton Ave E, Suite 900
Toronto, ON M4P 2Y3
Phone: 416-363-0321
Fax: 416-861-1291
Email: mail@ccla.org
Website: https://ccla.org

ReachOut Australia
PO Box Q501
Queen Victoria Building
NSW 1230
Phone: +61 2 8029 7777
Email: media@reachout.com
Website: https://au.reachout.com

Index

Picture Credits

All images in this book are in the public domain or have been supplied under license by © Shutterstock.com. The publisher credits the following image as follows: page 8: Krista Kennell, page 16: Ms Jane Campbell, page 24: Antonio Gravante.
© Dreamstime/page 6 above: Brianna Hunter, page 6 below: Rawpixelimages, page 7 above: Andrea de Martin, page 7 below Vladyslav Starozhylov.
To the best knowledge of the publisher, all images not specifically credited are in the public domain. If any image has been inadvertently uncredited, please notify the publisher, so that credit can be given in future printings.

Video Credits

Page 16 TED-Ed: http://x-qr.net/1HdU, page 25 PinkChicken42: http://x-qr.net/1GHY, page 32 The Better Adult Project: http://x-qr.net/1D3L, page 40 Lifehacker: http://x-qr.net/1Ghs, page 48 BreakthruInMarketing: http://x-qr.net/1EHd, page 55 BRIGHT SIDE: http://x-qr.net/1EbG

About the Author

Sarah Smith is a freelance writer currently living and working in the Boston area. She is also a board-certified Doctor of Physical Therapy, licensed by the Commonwealth of Massachusetts. She attended Boston University where she earned both her doctorate and, as an undergraduate, a Bachelor of Science in Health Studies.

Sarah has been writing for her entire life, and first became a published author at age 14, when she began contributing to a weekly column for her local newspaper. Since beginning her freelance writing career in earnest in 2014, Sarah has written over 1,500 articles and books. Her work covers a broad range of topics including psychology and relationships, as well as physical and mental health.

Additionally, she has over 15 years of professional experience working with typically developing and special-needs children, along with their families, in a variety of settings, including schools, pediatric hospitals, and youth-group fitness programs. She spent over 13 years working as a private nanny and babysitter for families in both her hometown of Yarmouth, Maine, as well as in and around the great city of Boston. Sarah also has experience tutoring and leading teens and young adults as part of a variety of clinical internship programs for physical therapy.